Bloomfield Township Public Library
Bloomfield Hills, Michigan 48302-2410

**A Gift from
The Friends of the Library
for the
Grand Opening Collection
2008**

SING and PLAY
PLANTS

PIE CORBETT

CHRYSALIS EDUCATION

LAVENDER'S BLUE

Lavender's blue, dilly dilly,
Lavender's green.
When I am King, dilly dilly,
You shall be Queen.

Lilies are white, dilly dilly,
Rosemary's green.
When you are King, dilly dilly,
I will be Queen.

Roses are red, dilly dilly,
Lavender's blue.
If you will have me, dilly dilly,
I will have you.

HOLLYHOCKS RED

Hollyhocks are red, dilly dilly,
Foxgloves are blue.
When you plant flowers, dilly dilly,
I will plant too.

Bulrushes are brown, dilly dilly,
Tulips are white.
Plants on the left, dilly dilly,
Plants on the right.

Poppies are red, dilly dilly,
Thyme and mint green.
When you get muddy, dilly dilly,
I will be clean.

Primroses are yellow, dilly dilly,
Sunflowers are gold.
Summer is hot, dilly dilly,
Winter is cold.

Forget-me-nots are blue, dilly dilly,
Snapdragons are red.
When we are done, dilly dilly,
It's time for bed.

FLOWERS

THINGS TO TALK ABOUT

Look at this flower.

How many petals are there?

What color are the leaves?

What does the stalk do?

Describe a flower you have seen.

petals

leaves

stalk

4

FLOWERS

THINGS TO DO

Make a beautiful tissue paper flower.

You need

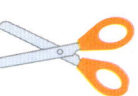

pencil   bowl   drinking straw   tissue paper   scotch tape   scissors

1. Draw around a small bowl and cut out lots of circles.

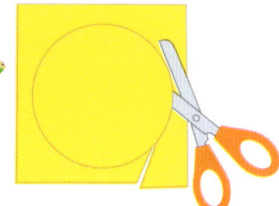

2. Pinch the center of all the circles and hold them together like this.

4. Open up the petals to make a beautiful flower.

3. Fix the paper flower to a drinking straw stalk by wrapping scotch tape around it.

5

FRUIT

ORANGES AND LEMONS

'Oranges and lemons,'
Say the bells of St. Clements.

'I owe you five farthings,'
Say the bells of St. Martins.

'When will you pay me?'
Say the bells of Old Bailey.

'When I grow rich,'
Say the bells of Shoreditch.

'When will that be?'
Say the bells of Stepney.

'I do not know,'
Says the great bell of Bow.

Here comes the candle to light you to bed.
Here comes the chopper to chop off your head.
Chip, chop, chip, chop, CHOP!

FRUIT

BANANAS AND LIME

Bananas and lime,
Now is your bedtime.

Currants and dates,
You must first wash the plates.

Cranberries are red,
You are my sleepyhead.

Apples and pears,
Let's climb up the stairs.

Mango and prune,
You can look at the moon.

Rhubarb and cream,
You can lie down and dream…

Here comes the moon to lighten the night.
Turn on the switch, to make the room bright.
Night, bright, night, bright, NIGHT!

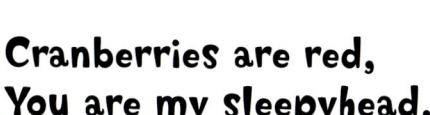

FRUIT

THINGS TO TALK ABOUT

Look at this apple.

What do you find inside a fruit?

What color is the skin?

Which fruits do you like to eat?

Which animals like eating fruit?

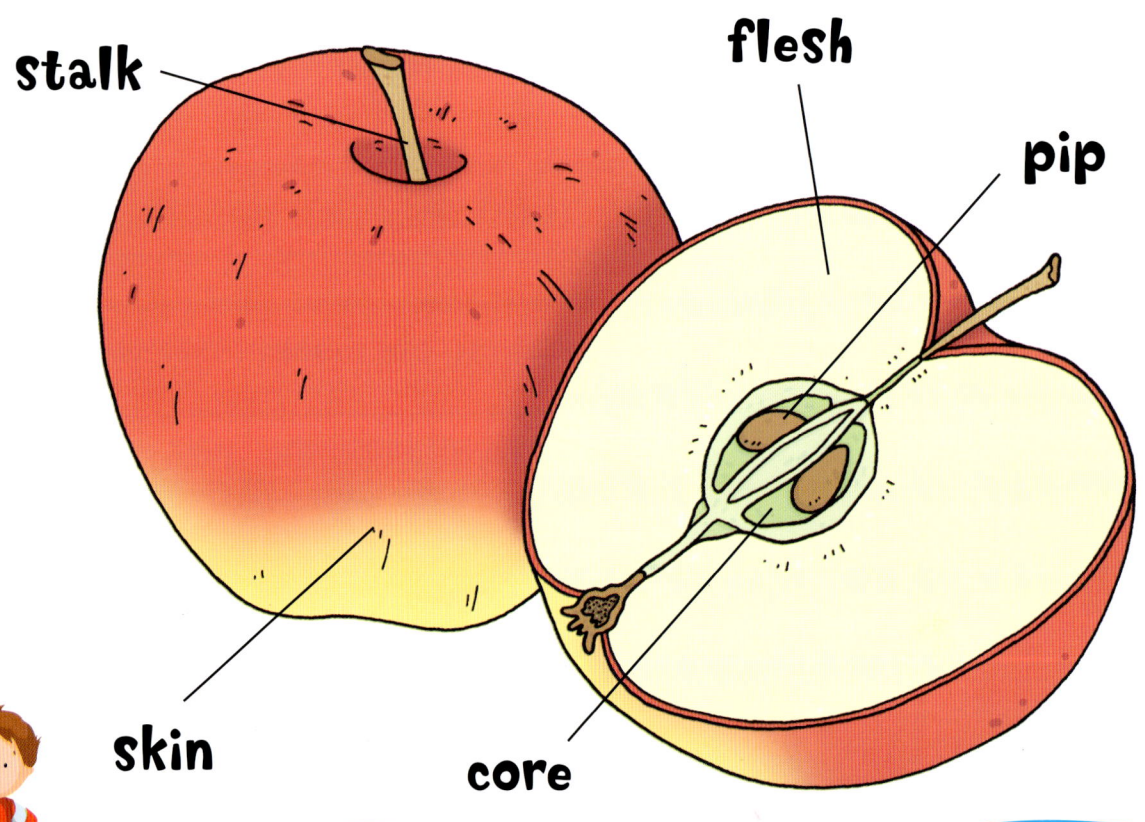

stalk

flesh

pip

skin

core

8

FRUIT

THINGS TO DO

Make a tasty fruit salad!

You need

a bowl 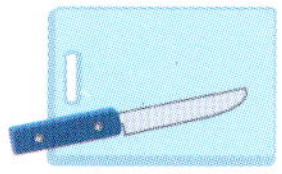   a chopping board       washed strawberries, peach, banana, apple, grapes    cream

1. Ask someone to help you prepare the fruits.

2. Cut them into small pieces.

3. Put the fruit into the bowl and mix it up.

4. Now it's ready to eat with cream or ice cream!

Knives are sharp! Make sure an adult helps you to cut up the fruit.

9

GARDENS

MARY, MARY

Mary, Mary, quite contrary,
How does your garden grow?

With silver bells and cockle shells,
And pretty maids all in a row, row, row.
And pretty maids all in a row!

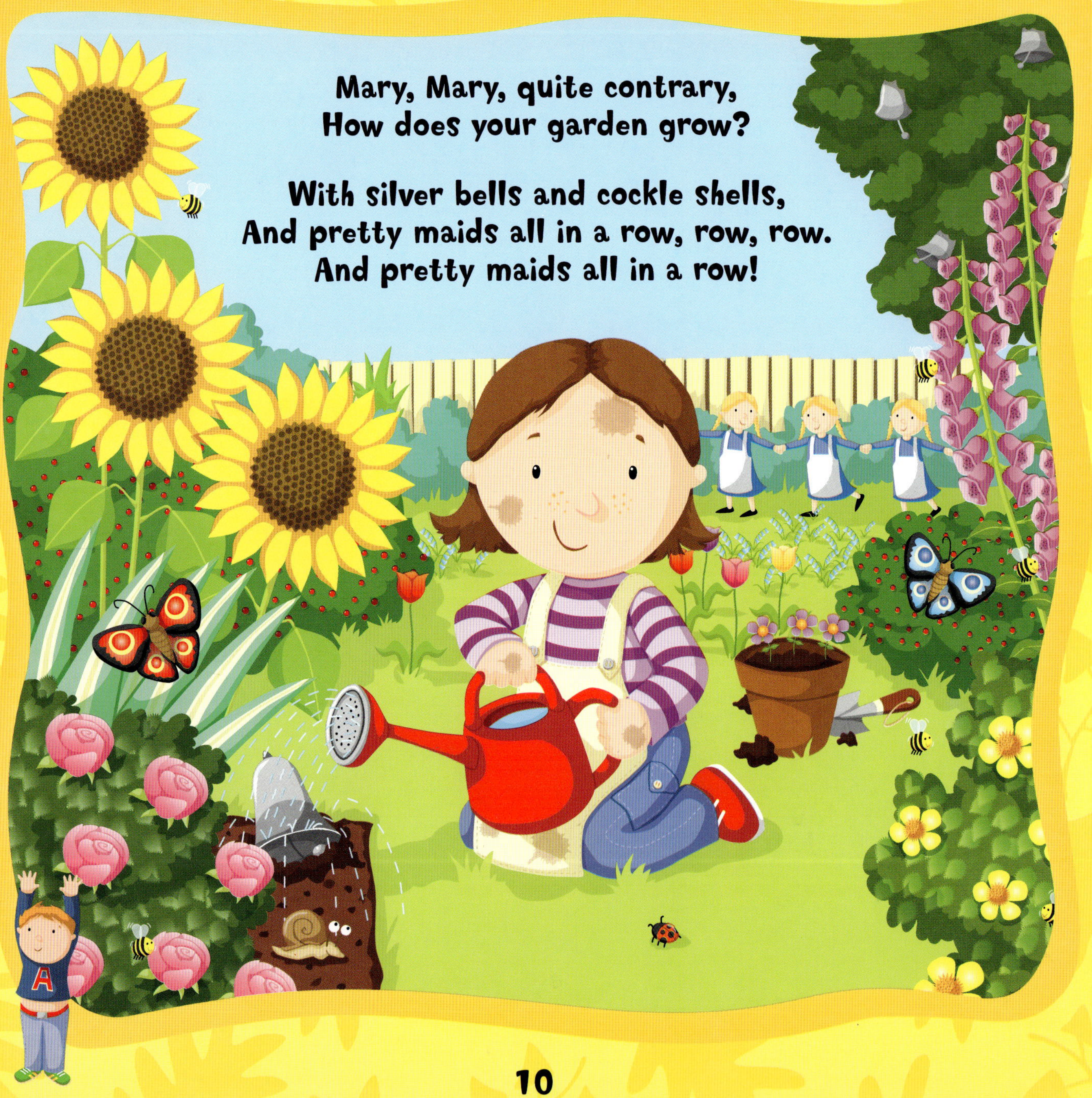

GARDENS

DAISY, DAISY

Daisy, Daisy, don't be lazy,
How do your poppies grow?

In sunlight bright, they grow their height,
And they bloom all in a row, row, row.
And they bloom all in a row!

Ruth, Ruth, tell the truth,
How do your apples grow?

Above your head, they're green and red,
And they blossom all in a row, row, row.
And they blossom all in a row!

Guy, Guy, don't be shy,
How do your carrots grow?

Look underground, it's where they're found,
And they shoot up all in a row, row, row.
And they shoot up all in a row!

GARDENS

THINGS TO TALK ABOUT

Look at these garden vegetables.

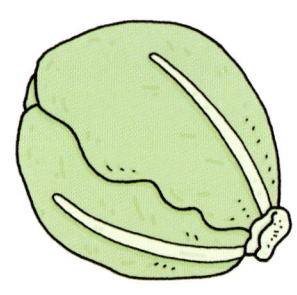
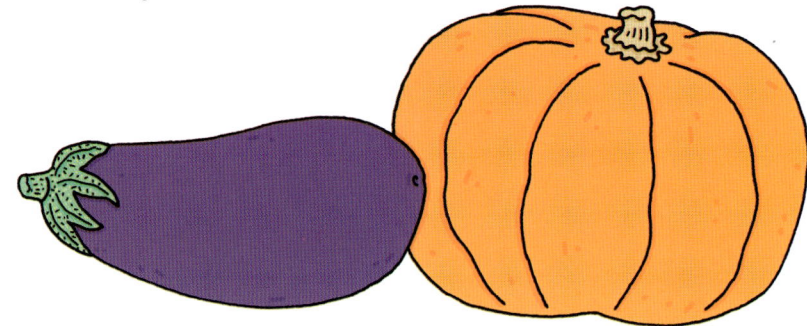

Do you know the names of these vegetables?

Which is the biggest?

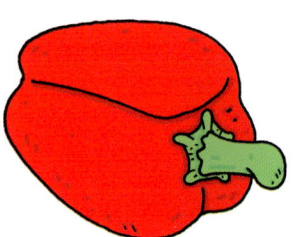

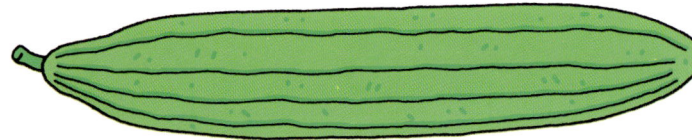

Which is the smallest?

Which of these vegetables have you eaten?

12

GARDENS

THINGS TO DO

Plant some colorful crocuses!

You need

a flowerpot   some soil   2 or 3 crocus bulbs   water

1. Pour the soil into the flowerpot.

2. Make 2 or 3 holes in the soil, about as long as your finger.

3. Place the bulbs in the holes and pat the soil back over them.

4. Water them so that the soil is wet.

5. Now place them in a sunny spot, water them regularly, and see what happens!

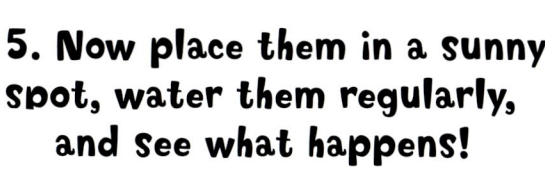

NUTS AND SEEDS

I HAD A LITTLE NUT TREE

I had a little nut tree,
Nothing would it bear.
But a silver nutmeg,
And a golden pear.

The King of Spain's daughter,
Came to visit me.
And all for the sake,
Of my little nut tree.

NUTS AND SEEDS

I HAD A LITTLE APPLE PIP

I had a little apple pip,
Growing in a pot.
When it grows into a tree,
We will eat the lot.

I planted a pumpkin seed,
Underneath the ground.
We watered it and waited,
While it grew so round.

Open up a coconut,
Give the milk a shake.
Serve it up, in a cup,
With a slice of cake.

I bit into a cherry,
The juice was oh-so sweet.
I almost cried, the stone inside,
Nearly broke my teeth!

NUTS AND SEEDS

THINGS TO TALK ABOUT

Look at these nuts and seeds.

Do you know their names?

Which one do you think is the heaviest?

Find out which are nuts and which are seeds.

NUTS AND SEEDS

THINGS TO DO

Make a cress man!

You need

cotton batting   an empty eggshell   egg cup   cress seeds   water   felt-tip pens

1. Place the cotton batting into the eggshell.

2. Add a little water to make it damp.

3. Sprinkle on some cress seeds.

4. Draw eyes, a nose, and a mouth on to the eggshell.

5. Place it on a sunny window sill and watch your cress man's hair grow!

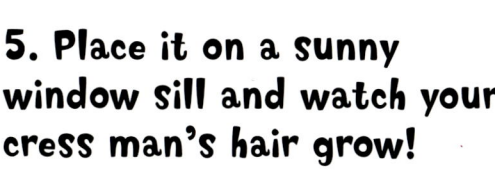

17

HERE WE GO ROUND THE MULBERRY BUSH

Here we go round the mulberry bush,
The mulberry bush, the mulberry bush.
Here we go round the mulberry bush,
On a cold and frosty morning.

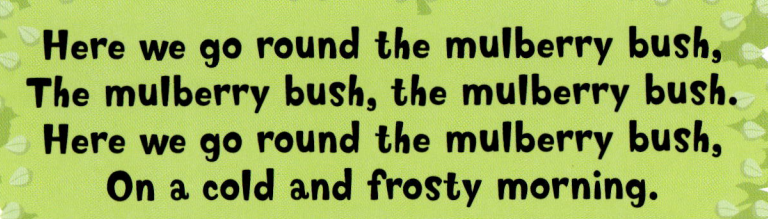

This is the way we wash our hands,
Wash our hands, wash our hands.
This is the way we wash our hands,
On a cold and frosty morning.

This is the way we wash our clothes,
Wash our clothes, wash our clothes.
This is the way we wash our clothes,
On a cold and frosty morning.

TREES

HERE WE GO ROUND THE OLD OAK TREE

Here we go round the old oak tree,
The old oak tree, the old oak tree.
Here we go round the old oak tree,
On a cool and chilly morning.

This is the way we stretch our branches,
Stretch our branches, stretch our branches.
This is the way we stretch our branches,
On a warm and sunny morning.

This is the way we grow our leaves,
Grow our leaves, grow our leaves.
This is the way we grow our leaves,
On a warm and sunny morning.

This is the way they fall and die,
Fall and die, fall and die.
This is the way they fall and die,
On a cool and chilly morning.

TREES

THINGS TO TALK ABOUT

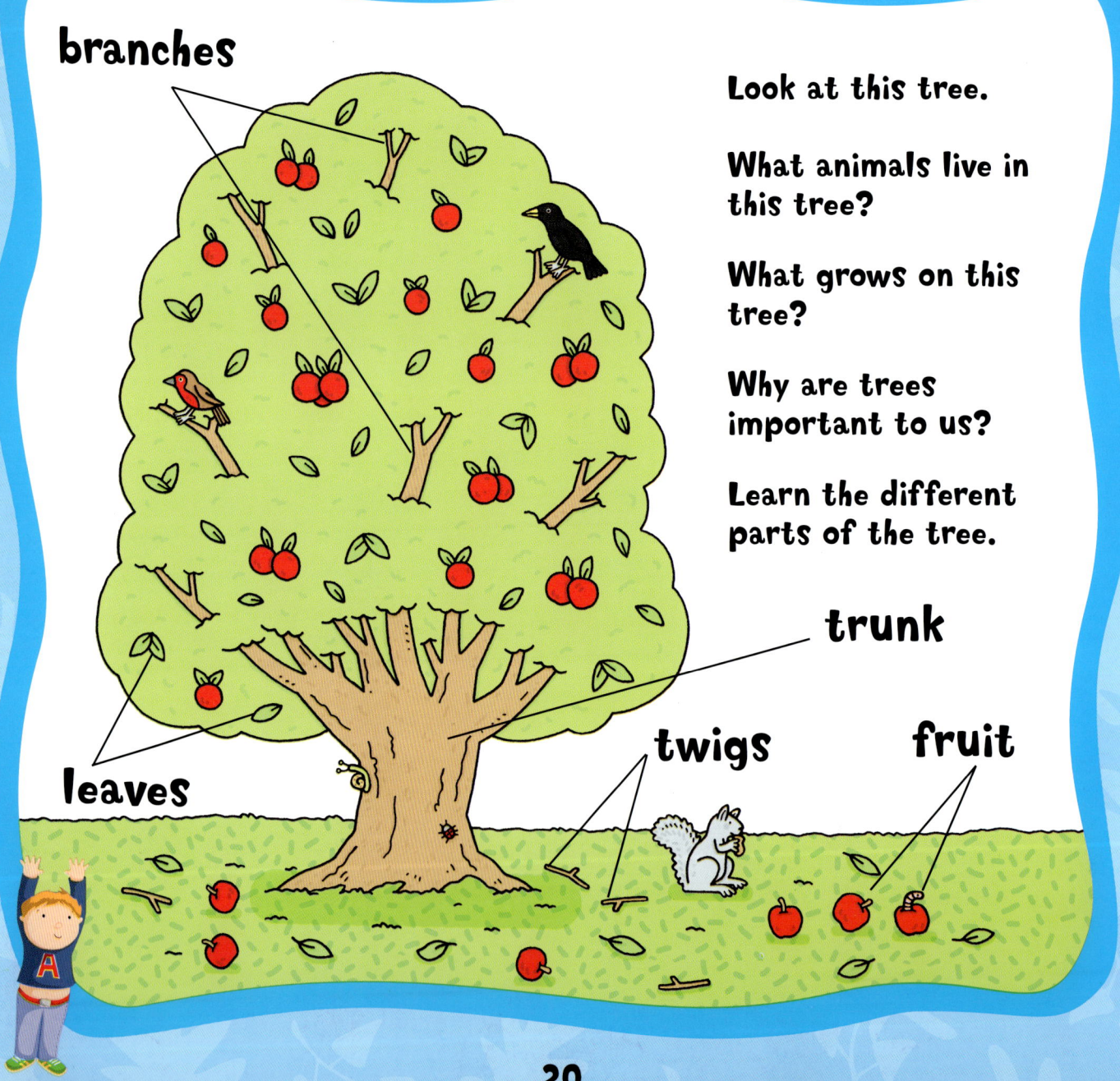

Look at this tree.

What animals live in this tree?

What grows on this tree?

Why are trees important to us?

Learn the different parts of the tree.

20

TREES

THINGS TO DO

Make a leaf picture!

You need

paints　　　　leaves　　　　paper　　　newspaper

1. Paint one side of your leaves.

2. Place them on a sheet of paper.

3. Lay another sheet of paper over the top and press down gently.

4. Carefully lift off the paper and leaves.

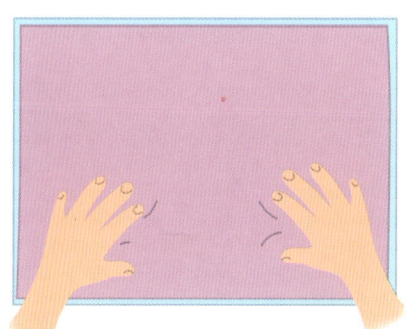

5. See the lovely picture you have made.

21

RHYME ACTIONS

Why not add some actions to the rhymes to make them fun?
Here are a few to get you started, but you could make up your own too!

HOW THE BOOK WORKS

The book is divided into five units: flowers, fruit, gardens, nuts and seeds, and trees. Each unit comprises four pages.

 The first page of each unit features a well-known nursery rhyme or traditional rhyme.

 On the second page of the unit, the words to the rhyme have been changed so that children can sing about a topic, learning basic information in an enjoyable way.

 The third page of the unit provides a topic for discussion where children can draw on their own experience and broaden their knowledge.

 The fourth page offers an activity for really involving the children.

TEACHERS' AND PARENTS' NOTES

Where you see an "open book" icon in the bottom right corner of a page, this indicates that there are further ideas, suggestions, or an explanation about the page's contents.

Page 12 Bring in a selection of vegetables for the children to look at. Ask the children to organize them into themes such as vegetables that grow under the ground and those that grow above ground, or by size, texture, weight, or color. A follow-up activity could be cutting up the vegetables to use for vegetable printing.

Page 13 Though this activity follows on from vegetables, it is important to emphasize that bulbs are not vegetables and should not be eaten! However, they are fun to grow. Choose the bulbs according to season and availability. Find a simple device, such as a card marked out in inches, to measure and record the bulbs' growth.

Index

Bulbs	13
Core	8
Cress man	17
Eating	8
Leaves	19-20, 21
Petals	4, 5
Pip	8, 15
Planting	3, 13, 15
Rhubarb	7
Seeds	16
Stalk	4, 5, 8
Things to do	5, 9, 13, 17, 21
Tree	14, 19-20
Vegetables	11-12

This U.S. edition copyright © 2006 Chrysalis Education
Published in conjunction with Chrysalis Books Group Plc.

International copyright reserved in all countries.
No part of this book may be reproduced in any form without written permission from the publisher.

Distributed in the United States by
Smart Apple Media
2140 Howard Drive West
North Mankato, Minnesota 56003

Library of Congress Control Number: 2004108783

ISBN 1-59389-207-1

Associate Publisher: Joyce Bentley
Project Editor: Debbie Foy
Editorial Assistant: Camilla Lloyd
Designer: Paul Cherrill
Illustrators: Ed Eaves, Jo Moore
and Molly Sage

Printed in China

10 9 8 7 6 5 4 3 2 1